potent punches

RED LIGHTNING BOOKS

potent punches

The Retro Guide to the Original Party Drink

Barbara Mealey

Foreword by Albert W. A. Schmid

This book is a publication of

Red Lightning Books
1320 East 10th Street
Bloomington, Indiana 47405 USA

redlightningbooks.com

ISBN 978-1-68435-014-8

1 2 3 4 5   23 22 21 20 19 18

Contents

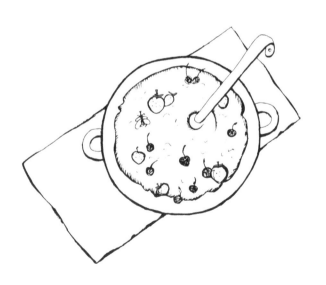

Foreword

Punch is an important part of my personal history. One of my favorite childhood beverages, during the sweltering Louisiana and Texas summers, was a nonalcoholic punch mixture primarily made from grape juice and lemonade. Punch was served at weddings, funerals, baptisms, and other family gatherings—not to mention church events. Many times, the punch would have ice or a frozen juice ring floating in the bowl to chill the punch. Now, one of my prized possessions is a rose-colored glass punch bowl with a gold-leaf rim that was owned by my grandparents and then my parents and that featured a mixed beverage at both of their weddings. I suspect that punch is important to many people's history.

Internationally, punch is an important drink. It's refreshing and fun and a communal drink that brings people together. Most cocktail books include at least one recipe for punch, and no church cookbook would be complete without one. Punch is a convenient party drink because there's no need for a bartender to mix and shake and stir—guests can simply fill a cup with ready-to-drink refreshment.

Punch, alcoholic or not, can include a plethora of ingredients, but is as easy to make as it is to drink! Many people know the Caribbean punch rhyme, "One of sour, two of sweet, three of strong, and four of weak" which is a fine drink recipe—one that I have used many times to make punch for a party. This recipe makes it easy to remember the components: one part sour (citrus fruit juice—lemon, lime, orange, grapefruit, etc.), two parts sugar, three parts spirit, and four parts water or nonalcoholic beverage.

The rhyming recipe seems to indicate that the original recipe for punch had four ingredients. However, the word "punch" comes from the Hindustani and Sanskrit word "pânc" (panch), which translated into English means "five," so the name "punch" is a direct reference to the number of ingredients in the original mixed beverage: (1) spirits, (2) water or milk, (3) lemon, (4) sugar, and (5) spice or cordial. Punch was introduced to England from India in the early seventeenth century, and its popularity spread throughout the vast domain of the British Empire—where the sun never set— from India to the Caribbean to Hong Kong to Australia. Punch is now served all over the world, and just as its popularity has expanded, the meaning of the word "punch" has expanded to include almost any mixture of potable liquids that contains fruit, fruit juice, or fruit-flavored juice . . . think Hawaiian Punch.

But, beware! Drinking alcoholic punch is like wading into the ocean. It seems harmless until you suddenly find yourself in over your head because the punch's sweet fruit flavors hide the alcohol. Many unwary partygoers have fallen victim to high school and college punch bowls spiked with a saboteur's rum, vodka, brandy, whiskey, or even mind-numbing high-proof grain-spirit and consumed more alcohol than they bargained for. Punch is a delightful addition to a party or get-together, so enjoy punch responsibly!

Cheers,
Albert W. A. Schmid
Greensboro, North Carolina

Foreword

potent punches

1

Entertaining

Beverages are as basic and essential to the cocktail party as the hors d'oeuvre. The bar gives the host a splendid opportunity to demonstrate his or her social expertise. The host should be knowledgeable about local drinking preferences, the liquors and wines of choice, and bar accessories.

As host you may hire a bartender, serve the guests yourself, or inform them that the bar is self-service. When entertaining fewer than twelve people, it is customary for the host to mix the cocktails. You will need a bartender when the guest list exceeds thirty-five unless you wish them to serve themselves. At the beginning of a large party you might circulate and ask a few guests if they would like to have a cocktail. These drinks should be presented to the guests on a tray, and thereafter, guests may be directed to the bar for beverages.

If you do not possess a built-in bar area, you can improvise. A fairly large table will do nicely. Otherwise, you could use serving carts, breakfast or card tables, or even something like orange crates or sawhorses with a piece of plywood laid across. In any case, cover the makeshift bar with a plastic covering that extends to the floor on at least three sides. This allows the surface to be sponged off as necessary and also permits storage of bottles and extra glassware to protect them from dust, soil, and breakage.

Ideally, the bar should be centrally located. To avoid congestion, however, it should not be placed too close to the kitchen and buffet table. If this is not practical, you may wish to have initial socializing apart from the bar, and serve punch or premixed "specialties of the house" until the buffet table is ready. At that time, invite guests to come to the bar.

Be sure to have nonalcoholic beverages on hand for those who do not wish to drink liquor. We suggest preparing one of the several delicious nonalcoholic punches included in chapter 5. Many sweet cocktails also taste fine without the addition of liquor. It would be thoughtful to suggest these to your guests. Or, if you prefer, you may offer soft drinks and fruit juices. It is customary to serve nonalcoholic drinks in the same glassware used for cocktails. Never encourage a guest to drink liquor against his wishes.

COFFEE AND TEA

Coffee and hot tea have a place alongside the food on every evening cocktail buffet. For an after-the-event soirée, have regular and decaffeinated versions of each available as soon as your guests come through the door. Espresso coffee is perfect with dessert, but regular coffee should be offered too. A twist of lemon peel in a cup of espresso will give it a more mellow flavor.

If you're expecting a crowd, you might borrow or rent party-sized coffee makers. Three pounds of regular-grind coffee will yield 100 large or 175 small cups. Tea may be served in a coffee maker if the group is large. Simply brew the tea in the pot. Pour boiling water over tea leaves wrapped in cheesecloth. Cover the pot, let the tea steep to the proper strength (five minutes for black tea and three minutes for green), and then remove the leaves. One pound of bulk tea will make 250 cups.

Offer your guests sugar, low-calorie sweetener, cream, and lemon slices studded with cloves. Provide two quarts of cream and two pounds of sugar for 100 cups. Use your best serving pieces together with silver spoons and a lemon fork.

If you do not want to serve coffee in cups or mugs of china, glass, or ceramic, use foam cups or sleeves, which provide insulation and are more comfortable to hold than paper cups. Espresso may be served in tiny foam or demitasse cups.

WINE

If wine is to be served, either as the beverage of the evening or for individual requests, offer still and sparkling wines of good quality. Typical wine apéritifs are Dubonnet, dry Madeira, sherry, and vermouth. These should be served well chilled. If you wish, dessert wines, such as sweet Madeira, port, sherry, and sauterne, and liqueurs may accompany the sweets. It is also a good idea to have iced lager or ale in case someone requests it.

COCKTAILS

A cocktail is only as perfect as its components. Use only good-quality ingredients; many people are able to discern inferior contents. Liquors should range from moderate to excellent in grade. Some brands of cocktail mixes are of superior flavor to others; experiment to find the types you prefer. We recommend that you keep a bartender's guide handy when preparing drinks for your guests. The recipes will give specific quantities, to which you should adhere.

Always measure accurately, use the required ingredients, and carefully observe the proper order and manner of blending them. Do not make substitutions unless you are fairly positive of the end result or are requested to do so by the guest.

The preparation of cocktails goes much more smoothly if you have a well-stocked bar. We have tried to provide a complete inventory, some of which you may not wish to include because of the season, the locale, or the type of party you are giving. The list does contain all of the essentials and should prove helpful.

PUNCH

Punch is one of the most popular social beverages. The punch bowl always has a festive air and it draws people together. If punch is the only beverage served, all labor involved with setting up the bar is eliminated. Therefore, punch is without equal when there are large numbers of guests. The punch for cocktail parties or buffets should be fairly potent—not the diluted version often served in the daytime. Included in chapter 5 are several nonalcoholic punch recipes, however, so you will not have to offer abstainers a soft drink or juice.

Many traditional punches contain fruit that has previously been marinated in liquor or sugared and left to stand for several days. Always use fresh fruits and juices rather than canned or frozen unless the punch recipe directs otherwise.

Chill all your ingredients well before mixing them in the punch bowl. The punch will be even more delicious, and the ice ring will not melt as readily. Large plastic containers are useful for storing the punch until serving.

A WELL-STOCKED BAR

Liquors

The well-stocked bar should include bourbon, blended and rye whiskies, scotch, vodka, gin, rum, tequila, and dry and sweet vermouth.

In addition, stock carbonated water, which dieters may drink on the rocks, tonic (particularly in summer), and one or two brands of soft drinks. Ice, a measuring glass and spoon, drinking glasses, and napkins are the only other absolute essentials. For an after-the-event soirée, you could prepare appropriate bulk quantities of screwdrivers and Bloody Marys, and offer no other alcoholic beverages. Allow two drinks per person, and mix three parts juice or mix to one part vodka.

Have coffee, tea, sparkling water, or soft drinks available for nondrinkers.

Set-ups

Purchase soda water, tonic water, ginger ale, colas, diet drinks, frozen limeade, lemonade and orange juice concentrates, lime juice, and tomato juice (with seasonings added) or a Bloody Mary mix (Mr. and Mrs. T is superior to the others we've tasted). Have available either the basic ingredients for preparing cocktails or good-quality whiskey sour, daiquiri, and Tom Collins mixes. In warm weather you might wish to have piña colada, chi-chi, and mai tai mixes as well.

A basic ingredient in piña coladas and chi-chis prepared without a mix is coconut cream. Coconut milk is a part of many other tropical drinks.

Coconut Milk and Cream

Pour boiling milk over an equal amount of grated coconut, and let stand for 25 minutes. Strain the liquid, pressing the coconut with a spoon or your hands to yield a maximum amount of milk (about one-third of the milk will saturate the coconut and cannot be readily squeezed out). Refrigerate the coconut milk for several hours. A thick creamy substance, which is coconut cream, will form on top. Skim this cream off the top of the coconut milk. Refrigerate both until using.

Garnishes and Flavorings

Lime slices or wedges, pitted olives, cocktail onions, maraschino cherries with stems, bitters, and grenadine are standard cocktail accompaniments. You will need cocktail-length bamboo skewers or long, colorful plastic picks to spear lemon, orange, and lime slices, pineapple cubes or wedges, strawberries, grapes, and perhaps mint leaves. If you use bottled fruit, drain, rinse, pat dry, and refrigerate in a covered container until ready to use.

Lemon peel is often added to drinks such as bourbon and water. To make attractive twists, use a vegetable peeler make thin spirals of peel with little or no white skin attached. Twist the lemon strip over the surface of the drink and then drop the peel into the glass. The lemon oil adds flavor and aroma. When cucumber rind is called for, cut thin slices of fresh rind and place on the edge of the glass.

Sweeteners

Use confectioner's or superfine granulated sugar for quick dissolving. Or, if you prefer, use a simple syrup that has been prepared ahead of time. When drinks contain sweeteners, pour in the liquor last.

Ice

Have plenty on hand. If freezer space allows, make ice cubes for several days before the party. Plan to use three regular-size cubes per drink. Use whole cubes for stirred drinks, cracked ice for shaker drinks, and crushed ice for frozen drinks. Store extra ice in insulated picnic chests underneath or adjacent to the bar.

ICE MOLDS

There are several ways to make ice molds to float in a punch bowl. All are successful if instructions are followed carefully.

1. Fill the mold with tap water. Empty this water into another bowl and set aside for fifteen minutes to deaerate. Pour one-fourth of the water into the mold and freeze. Add one-fourth more water to the ice and freeze. Lay garnishes on top, pour remaining water over all, and freeze.

2. Use distilled or boiled tap water. Pour half of the water into the mold and freeze. Then place garnishes on the ice, cover with remaining water, and freeze.

3. Freeze part of the actual punch except for last-minute ingredients, such as sparkling water. Add garnishes, fill to the top with punch, and freeze. This method insures that the punch will not become diluted.

Some attractive garnishes include strawberries, cherries, pineapple, grapes, orange, lemon or lime slices, mint, ivy, and fresh flowers (either alone or with greenery).

To unmold ice rings, dip the mold in hot water until the ice slips out easily. Place the ring in very cold punch, decorative side up. It is advisable to prepare two or more ice rings for the punch bowl, replacing them as necessary.

Punch Bowls
Punch bowls usually are made of glass or silver and come with matching cups. For a large group or when the punch is in cocktail form, Old-Fashioned glasses are a useful substitute for the traditional punch cup. Since the ladle is often made of heavy glass or silver, you might wish to purchase an inexpensive plastic one that is lightweight and easy to manipulate. If the punch is hot, you must provide insulated cups. Punch, Styrofoam, tea, or coffee cups may be used.

Punch bowl placement is a matter of preference. The bowl may be at either end of the buffet table if it does not crowd the food trays and clutter the overall appearance of the table. Ideally, however, it should be situated by itself on a round table, with a cloth draped to the floor. Remove all chairs from around the punch table, allowing enough room for guests to serve themselves from any direction.

For a special decorative touch you may frost the punch bowl. Beat one egg white with one tablespoon of water. Brush a band of this mixture in any width desired around the outside rim of the bowl. Sprinkle wax paper with regular or superfine granulated sugar. Colored sugars that harmonize with the punch are quite festive. Roll the wet rim in the sugar to frost. After about twenty minutes, recoat with sugar, and allow to air dry for several hours.

Glassware

Glassware for serving beverages should be assembled and cleaned several days prior to the party and stored under cover. It is wise to have at least two glasses per person, as many will forget where they put down the empty one or may wish to change their drink selection. You will need 8-ounce Old-Fashioned glasses for on-the-rock drinks such as martinis, Manhattans, and the like. This size will serve also for liqueurs over ice. The 14-ounce double Old-Fashioned is perfect for highballs, Bloody Marys, tropical drinks, and nonalcoholic beverages. You may wish to invest in beer mugs or goblets that are also used for cold weather concoctions. Large, tulip-shaped wine glasses are suitable for whiskey and scotch sours, but the small Old-Fashioned glasses serve just as well.

Serving beverages in glassware at a large gathering necessitates dishwashing during the party to keep the glasses clean. Keep in mind that it is perfectly correct to use disposable plastic glasses for mixed drinks or to use glassware for the first round and have plastic in reserve. Beer and wine, however, are best served in authentic glass. If you decide you want to use glassware, either buy the inexpensive variety, which is usually thick and break resistant, or rent what you need. Rental is not costly and is convenient if you do not entertain frequently. If you have basic glassware and need to fill in, you may do so with rental or plastic.

In the summertime, try frosting thin-walled glasses for a cooling effect. Frosting may be done by placing glasses in the refrigerator, freezer, or ice chest. Or, you may dip glasses in slightly beaten egg whites, roll them in granulated sugar, and then air-dry.

Bar Equipment

    Ice bucket and tongs
    Ice pick and/or ice crusher
    Cutting board and a thin, sharp knife
    Corkscrew
    Bottle opener
    Long bar spoon
    Lemon stripper or vegetable peeler
    Juicer for lemons and limes
    Strainer
    1-oz. mini-measuring cup or medicine
       glass for measuring (preferable to
       shot glass)
    Shot glasses that measure accurately
       according to size jigger called for
       in recipe
    Measuring cup with ½-ounce markings
    Shaker with glass stirrer

Glassware
Trays for clean and used glassware
Pitcher of cold water
Pitcher for mixing multiple servings
of a drink at one time
Towels
Cocktail napkins (must accompany
each drink served)
Straws and stirrers
Blender
Waste container

Measurements

Accurate measurement is essential when mixing cocktails and other beverages. The difference between ½ ounce and 1 ounce is 100 percent. Use a 1-oz. mini-measuring cup or medicine glass to measure accurately when mixing cocktails. These cups are marked in fractions of ounces, teaspoons, and tablespoons and in milliliters. The following list of measurements is a standard guide to good bartending.

1 dash = ⅟₁₆ teaspoon
1 teaspoon = ⅛ ounce
1 tablespoon = ½ ounce

1 small jigger (or pony) = 1 ounce

1 jigger (standard) = 1 ½ ounces

1 large jigger = 2 ounces

1 quart (British) = 40 ounces

1 bottle vermouth = 30 ounces

1 bottle champagne = 24 to 26 ounces
    or 6 champagne glasses

1 magnum champagne = 52 ounces
    or 14 to 16 champagne glasses

1 bottle wine (⅘ quart) = 6 wine glasses

The following is a comparison of six of the most common bottle sizes in US measurements and their near equivalents in standard metric sizes:

US	Metric
miniature (1.6 oz.)	50 ml. (1.7 oz.)
half pint (8 oz.)	200 ml. (6.8 oz.)
pint (16 oz.)	500 ml. (16.9oz.)
fifth (⅘ quart) (25.6 oz.)	750 ml. (25.4 oz.)
quart (32 oz.)	1 liter (33.8 oz.)
half gallon (64 oz.)	1.75 liter (59.2 oz.)

A fifth yields approximately sixteen drinks.

One American quart or one liter will serve about twenty cocktails, using one standard jigger per drink. You may figure on two drinks per person for cocktails before dinner or three to five drinks, some nonalcoholic, per person for an all-evening affair.

Here is a general guide of quantities to have on hand for various numbers of guests based on three alcoholic drinks per person, using one standard jigger per drink. Distribution of liquors will depend upon local drinking preferences.

Guests Total	US Quarts or Liters	Ice Cubes	Bourbon	Scotch	Gin	Vodka
20	4	180 (12 lb.)	2	1 pt.	1 pt.	1
35	6	315 (20 1b.)	2	1	1	2
50	8	450 (28 lb.)	3	1	2	2
75	12	675 (42 lb.)	4	2	3	3

One pound of ice cubes is needed for five drinks with three cubes in each. One fifth or one 750 ml. bottle of Bloody Mary mix will yield five to six drinks, and one quart or one liter of orange juice is sufficient for seven screwdrivers, using a standard jigger for measurement. Two

Potent Punches

28-ounce bottles of soda water are sufficient for nine scotch- or bourbon-and-sodas. Soft drinks are usually served in 8-ounce glasses.

2

Cocktails and Liqueurs

Planter's Punch

THE UNIVERSITY CLUB OF INDIANA UNIVERSITY
Yield: 1 serving

1 lg. jigger orange juice
1 lg. jigger pineapple juice
1 lg. jigger lime juice
1 ¼ oz. white rum
1 ¼ oz. amber rum
½ oz. egg white
¾ oz. grenadine
1 oz. Jamaican rum

Combine all ingredients except grenadine and Jamaican rum, and shake well. Pour into tall glass filled with ice. Top with grenadine and Jamaican rum. Garnish with fruit (optional).

Piña Colada

BARBARA MEALEY
Yield: 16 4-ounce servings

1 c. coconut cream, chilled
2 c. pineapple juice, sweetened or
    unsweetened, chilled
1 ⅓ c. light rum, chilled
Superfine granulated sugar (optional)
4 c. ice, cubes or crushed

Combine half of all ingredients in blender. Blend on high speed until well mixed. Repeat with the second half. Serve in frosted glasses with a pineapple spear and a straw.

Note: May be placed in chilled punch bowl with fresh pineapple garnish and ice ring.

Strawberry Daiquiri

PAT CONNOLLY
Yield: 6 4-ounce servings

1 6-oz. can frozen lemonade
6 oz. rum
1 pt. fresh strawberries, cleaned
5 ice cubes (approximately)
HINT: Use the lemonade can to measure
the rum.

Place all ingredients in blender and mix well.
Serve in frosted Old-Fashioned glasses.

Nancy Petry's Rum Punch

MARION HELMEN
Yield: 9 4-ounce servings

> 1 6-oz. can frozen orange juice
> 1 6-oz. can frozen lemonade
> 6 oz. white rum
> 18 oz. water
> HINT: Use the lemonade can to measure
> the rum and water.

Combine all ingredients and freeze in plastic container for 8 to 10 hours. Scoop out and serve in small Old-Fashioned glasses with spoon or straws.

Potent Punches

Peach Delight

MARION HELMEN
Yield: 7 4-ounce servings

1 6-oz. can frozen limeade concentrate
6 oz. rum
1 ½ c. water (approximately)
4 peaches, peeled, pitted, cut up

Place all ingredients in the blender and blend until peaches are puréed. Freeze. Scoop out and serve in small Old-Fashioned glasses.

Peach Fluff

PAT CONNOLLY
Yield: 5 4-ounce servings

1 6-oz. can frozen lemonade
6 oz. vodka
2 whole peaches, fresh, unpeeled, but pitted
5 ice cubes (approximately)

Place all ingredients into the blender and mix well. Serve in frosted Old-Fashioned glasses.

Bloody Marys

SONIA MCCORMICK
Yield: 15 4-ounce servings

½ fifth of vodka
1 jigger Worcestershire sauce
1 jigger lemon juice
3 dashes Tabasco, or to taste
1 46-oz. can tomato juice

Combine all ingredients and stir well.
Pour into glasses filled with ice.

Bloody Mary Frappé

MARION HELMEN
Yield: 6 servings

1 25.6-oz. bottle Bloody Mary mix
1 c. vodka

Combine and pour into 13 × 9-inch stainless
steel pan. Cover with plastic wrap. Freeze until firm. Scoop into sherbet or plastic glasses.
Garnish with celery leaves. Serve with spoons
or straws.

Potent Cocktail

ANONYMOUS
Yield: 14 4-ounce servings

> 1 qt. cranberry juice
> 12 oz. bourbon whiskey
> 1 12-oz. can frozen lemonade concentrate

Freeze to slushy consistency in ice trays. Serve with short plastic straws in small frosted cocktail glasses.

Whiskey Sour

MARY CONNEALLY
Yield: 4 to 6 servings

1 6-oz. can frozen lemonade
    concentrate
6 oz. club soda
6 oz. whiskey

Put above ingredients in blender.
Add ice and blend.

Sweet 'n' Sour Fizz

SONIA MCCORMICK
Yield: 3 4-ounce servings

6 oz. gin
3 oz. sweet and sour bar mix
4 ½ oz. milk
Dash of orange blossom water
    (available at Middle Eastern groceries)

Fill blender half full with chopped ice and
rest of ingredients. Blend until ice is melted.
Pour into small frosted glasses.

Potent Punches

Lo-Cal Cocktail

SONIA MCCORMICK
Yield: 4 servings

- 1 oz. lime juice
- 1 oz. lemon juice
- ¾ c. gin
- ¾ c. milk
- ½ c. crushed ice
- 2 egg whites
- ¾ oz. low calorie sweetener
- 6–8 drops orange blossom water

Place all ingredients into a blender in order listed. Blend well.

Sangría

SONIA MCCORMICK
Yield: 13 4-ounce servings

   1 fifth very dry Spanish burgundy
   ½ fifth champagne
   4 oz. brandy
   2 each: oranges, lemons, and limes,
      quartered

Squeeze citrus fruits and pour into a pitcher.
Add burgundy and brandy and chill well. Just
before serving add champagne and ice. Serve
in tall glasses of ice. Garnish with fruit.

Champagne Dazzlers

JERRI BURKE

Yield: 6 to 8 servings

   1 fifth champagne
   1 6-oz. can frozen lemonade concentrate
   1 c. orange juice
   6 oz. club soda
   6 oz. vodka
   2 c. ice cubes

Blend all ingredients except champagne in blender. Pour 1 oz. champagne in each wine glass and fill with blender mixture.

San Francisco Cocktail

DRUSCILLA DEFALQUE
Yield: 10 to 12 servings

2 fifths white port
1 c. white rum
Juice of 4 lemons
Fresh strawberries or cherries

Chill port. Marinate fresh fruit in rum and lemon juice. When ready to serve, mix together well and serve over ice cubes.

Mexican Patriot Cocktail

JEAN HORNBACK AND BARBARA MEALEY
Yield: 8 to 10 servings

1 pt. tequila
3 6-oz. cans frozen limeade
    concentrate, undiluted
8–10 mandarin orange slices or
    other yellow fruit
4 oz. green grapes or green
    maraschino cherries
4 oz. red maraschino cherries

Pour 1 c. tequila and half of concentrate
(9 oz.) into blender; fill three-quarters full
with ice. Blend for 1 minute. Put in pitcher
and repeat with remaining tequila and
concentrate. Refrigerate or freeze if not
to be used immediately. Serve in cocktail
glasses with a straw. Add to each glass
1 grape, 1 orange slice, and 1 cherry (well-
drained and rinsed) to represent the colors
of the Mexican flag.

Pisco Sour

BARBARA MEALEY
Yield: 6 servings

> 2 egg whites, room temperature
> 3 T. superfine granulated sugar
> 1 ½ c. pisco (Peruvian brandy)
> 3 T. lemon or lime juice, fresh

Place all ingredients into blender. Blend at high speed until quite frothy. Pour into small cocktail glasses and serve over ice. Pisco is quite potent; you may wish to decrease the amount.

Potent Punches

Sangría Blanco

MARILYN LINDSETH
Yield: 8 servings

  1 fifth dry white wine
  1 T. lime juice
  1 c. pineapple juice
  ⅓ c. orange or grapefruit juice
  3 T. lemon juice
  ¼ c. superfine granulated sugar
  1 7-oz. bottle carbonated water

Combine first 6 ingredients in a pitcher. Add ice cubes and stir until well-chilled. Gently stir in carbonated water. Garnish with lemon, lime, and orange slices. Serve over ice in glasses.

Frozen Margaritas

GOURMET GROUP
Yield: 6 to 8 servings

    1 6-oz. can lemonade concentrate
    4 oz. tequila
    3 T. fresh lime juice
    2 oz. Triple Sec

Put all ingredients in blender. Add enough
ice cubes to make a slushy mixture when
blended (approximately 1 tray).

Potent Punches

Margaritas La Paz

MIRIAM HOLDEN
Yield: 5 to 6 servings

    2 oz. triple sec
    5 oz. tequila
    1 6-oz. can daiquiri mix
    1 T. lime sherbet
    1 c. crushed ice
    1 t. plus a little more egg white

Put everything into a blender and blend at high speed for a few seconds. Rub edge of glasses with lime or lemon and dip into coarse salt before pouring drinks into them.

Coffee Liqueur

JACKIE KALSBECK AND
MARGARET LAUTZENHEISER
Yield: ½ gallon

    1 fifth brandy
    2 c. water
    1 2-oz. jar instant coffee
    4 c. sugar
    1 whole vanilla bean, split

Bring water to a boil. Stirring constantly, slowly add coffee and then sugar. Cool. Cut vanilla bean into little pieces with scissors after splitting. Put water mixture into ½-gallon bottle. Add vanilla bean and brandy. Cover tightly and shake well. Let brew for 30 days, shaking every few days. On 30th day, strain liqueur through fine strainer or cheesecloth. To serve, pour over ice and top with cream, if you like. Also delicious over ice cream.

Troika Special

NANCY MEADOWS
Yield: 1 serving

1 oz. lemon juice
1 oz. vodka
1 small jigger of Tia Maria or other
coffee liqueur
1 small jigger Cointreau or other
orange liqueur

Combine all ingredients and serve over ice.
For more servings increase all ingredients
equally.

Frosted Black Russian

BEVERLY MURPHY
Yield: 1 serving

1 oz. Kahlúa
3 oz. vodka
3 ice cubes, crushed

Combine Kahlúa and vodka, add crushed ice, and serve in small, chilled brandy snifter and with a cocktail straw.

Potent Punches

Crème de Menthe

JACKIE KALSBECK
Yield: 1 quart

- 1 c. water
- 2 c. vodka
- 1 c. sugar
- ¼ c. white corn syrup
- 6 drops oil of mint, not essence
  (sold in drugstores)

Boil sugar and water until sugar is dissolved. Add rest of ingredients and bottle. Ready to drink in approximately 1 week.

Note: May add green food coloring if desired.

3

Potent Punches

Ooh-La-La Champagne

DRUSCILLA DEFALQUE
Yield: 105 4-ounce servings

> 1 12-oz. can frozen orange juice
>   concentrate
> 1 6-oz. can frozen limeade concentrate
> 1 pt. apricot brandy, chilled
> 2 gal. champagne, chilled
> 2 qt. soda water, chilled
> 2 qt. 7-Up, chilled

Combine orange juice and limeade concentrates with brandy in punch bowl. Just

before serving add champagne, soda, and
7-Up. Blend together. Float a decorative ice
ring in the punch bowl.

Magnificent Punch
DONNA WORTH
Yield: 44 6-ounce servings

> 1 qt. vodka
> 1 qt. light sherry (not too dry)
> ½ c. maraschino cherry juice
> 1 c. curaçao
> 4 qt. or 5 fifths champagne, chilled
> 2 qt. club soda, chilled
>   (2 28-oz. bottles plus 1 c.)

Combine first 4 ingredients and pour into
punch bowl. At serving time carefully pour
in champagne and soda.

Note: Punch is extremely smooth but very
potent.

Champagne Punch

PHYLLIS COCKERILL
Yield: 28 4-ounce servings

    1 16-oz. pkg. frozen sliced strawberries
    ½ c. lime juice
    2 ½ c. lemon juice
    2 T. liquid sugar substitute, to taste
    1 qt. dry white wine
    2 ¼ qt. champagne

Mix. Pour in champagne last. Float lemon slices on top.

Champagne Punch

SONIA MCCORMICK
Yield: 48 4-ounce servings

- ½ c. sugar
- ½ c. lemon juice
- 1 c. maraschino cherry juice
- 1 pt. brandy
- 4 bottles champagne, chilled
- 2 qt. soda water, chilled

Add sugar to lemon and cherry juices, stirring until sugar is dissolved. Add brandy. Pour into punch bowl. Add large ice ring or block of ice. Gently pour champagne and soda water over ice.

Champagne Punch

EVELYN WELLMAN
Yield: 24 punch cups

> 1 bottle champagne, pink or white
> 1 qt. 7-Up
> 1 bottle sauterne wine

Mix champagne, 7-Up, and sauterne. Pour over ice block in punch bowl. If white champagne is used, add a few drops of grenadine for color.

Champagne Rouge Punch

ANONYMOUS
Yield: 25 cups

8 c. cranberry juice cocktail
1 6-oz. can frozen orange juice concentrate
1 6-oz. can frozen pineapple juice
    concentrate
1 6-oz. can frozen lemonade concentrate
2 c. brandy
2 fifths champagne, chilled

Combine cranberry juice, concentrates, and brandy in a large punch bowl. Add a block of ice. Just before serving slowly add chilled champagne.

Note: For nonalcoholic punch substitute 2 c. grape juice and 2 qt. ginger ale for brandy and champagne.

Vin Rouge Sparkling Punch

DRUSCILLA DEFALQUE
Yield: 100 4-ounce servings

    3 gal. dry red wine, well-chilled
    2 doz. lemons, sliced
    3 doz. oranges, sliced
    3 c. sugar
    1 gal. soda water

Place orange and lemon slices in large punch bowl and cover with sugar. Let stand for at least 1 hour. When ready to serve carefully pour wine and soda water over fruits. Add ice ring in which more lemons and oranges have been frozen.

Moselle Punch

MIRIAM HOLDEN
Yield: 20 to 30 servings

> 6 oranges, thinly sliced
> 2 fifths moselle wine
> 1 c. superfine granulated sugar
> 3 fifths champagne

Place orange slices in bowl and sprinkle with sugar. Pour 1 bottle of wine over fruit and let stand at least 1 hour. Pour over block of ice in punch bowl. Add remaining wine and champagne.

Syllabub

GOURMET GROUP

Yield: 18 4-ounce servings

2 c. medium-dry white wine
4–5 T. lemon rind, freshly grated
⅓ c. lemon juice
1 c. sugar
3 c. milk
2 c. light cream
4 egg whites, stiffly beaten with ½ c. sugar
Nutmeg

Combine first 3 ingredients. Add 1 c. sugar, stir, and then let rest until sugar dissolves. Combine milk and cream in mixing bowl and add wine mixture. Beat with rotary beater or wire whisk until frothy. Pour into punch bowl. Add puffs of beaten egg whites and sprinkle with nutmeg.

Limón y Cerveza

BARBARA MEALEY
Yield: 12 servings

2 c. sugar
2 c. water
1 ¾ c. lemon juice (reserve rinds)
¾ c. grapefruit juice
2 12-oz. bottles light beer
Clove-studded lemon slices

Mix sugar and water and bring to boiling point. Add lemon rinds from all lemons squeezed. Cover and let stand for 5 minutes. Remove rinds and cool. Add lemon and grapefruit juices. Pour into punch bowl and add ice ring. Just before serving slowly add beer. Float lemon slices on top.

Holiday Punch

DOROTHY MORRISON
Yield: 12 to 14 servings

> 1 qt. vanilla ice cream
> ½ fifth bourbon

Soften ice cream. Add bourbon and beat with mixer until lumps of ice cream disappear. Pour into punch bowl (or large pitcher) and serve. May garnish with holly which has been well rinsed and chilled.

Strawberry Punch

DONNA WORTH
Yield: 20 6-ounce servings

> 1 10-oz. pkg. frozen strawberries
> 1 8-oz. can crushed pineapple (canned in own juice; do not drain)
> 1 7-oz. can frozen lemonade
> 3 28-oz. bottles ginger ale
> 2–2 ½ c. vodka

Blend in blender the strawberries, pineapple, and lemonade. Add ginger ale and vodka. Vodka can be omitted, and the punch is still very refreshing and good for luncheons, showers, etc.

Fish House Punch

GOURMET GROUP
Yield: 35 4-ounce servings

¾–1 lb. sugar
Cold water, enough to dissolve sugar
1 qt. lemon juice, strained
2 qt. Jamaican rum
1 qt. cognac
½ c. peach brandy

Stir lemon juice into dissolved sugar. Pour over ice in punch bowl. Add in order rum, cognac, and peach brandy. Allow punch to sit for several hours before serving, stirring occasionally.

Bourbon Bellissima

DRUSCILLA DEFALQUE
Yield: 110 4-ounce servings

> 1 ¼ c. red maraschino cherry juice
> 2 12-oz. cans frozen lemonade, diluted
> 2 12-oz. cans frozen orange juice, diluted
> 2 fifths bourbon, chilled
> 1 gal. ginger ale, chilled
> 2 qt. soda water, chilled

Blend well cherry juice, lemonade, and orange juice. Chill. Before serving add bourbon, ginger ale, and soda water to juice mixture in punch bowl. Float an ice ring encasing cherries and slices of orange and lemon.

Whiskey Sour Punch

JACKIE KAISBECK
Yield: 20 5-ounce servings

3 16-oz. bottles Holland House Whiskey
    Sour mix
1 3-oz. pkg. lemonade mix
1 qt. 7-Up
Blended whiskey, to taste (1 c. to 1 fifth)

Chill liquid ingredients. Combine all but the
7-Up. Just before serving, splash with 7-Up.
Add ice ring which has orange slices and red
maraschino cherries frozen within. Garnish
punch with strips of orange rinds.

Danish West Indian Punch

JOHANNES RASMUSSEN
Yield: 26 4-ounce servings

10 oz. fresh lime juice
10 oz. sugar
1 fifth heavy Jamaican rum
1 fifth light rum
½ fifth Cointreau
½ fifth brandy
½ bottle sweet vermouth
2 t. Angostura bitters

Add all to equal quantity of ice and water.
Best made in advance, using all ice and allowing it to melt. More lime juice or sugar may be added to suit individual tastes. Very potent.

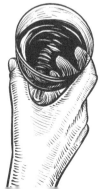

Frozen Daiquiri Punch

BARBARA MEALEY
Yield: 12 to 18 servings

> 1 16-oz. bottle Daiquiri mix
> 6–8 T. superfine granulated sugar
> 2 ½ c. light rum
> ½ c. orange liqueur
> 1 28-oz. bottle soda water, chilled
>   (optional)

Combine mix and sugar; stir until dissolved. Add liquors to this mixture and refrigerate until well-chilled (3 to 4 hours). Blend part of this liquid mixture in blender with a few ice cubes until slushy. Pour out of blender into bowl and refrigerate. Continue blending until all of liquor mixture is used. Remove from refrigerator just before serving and pour into a punch howl. Insert ice mold garnished with mint. Add soda water, if desired.

Cranberry Punch

GOURMET GROUP
Yield: 12 servings

6 c. cranberry juice cocktail
1 c. frozen orange juice
3 T. lemon juice
1¼ c. pineapple juice
2 c. water

Rum to taste or 1 part rum to 4 parts punch
Mix in order given. Pour over ice block in
punch bowl.

Potent Punches

4

Cold Weather Concoctions

Irish Coffee

WANDA NASSER
Yield: 1 serving

> 1 ½ oz. Irish whiskey
> 1 t. sugar
> Coffee, strong, hot
> Whipped cream, chilled
> Nutmeg

Pour Irish whiskey into a pre-warmed
(not necessary, but nice) 8-ounce cup or mug.
Add sugar and fill to within ½ inch of the top

with coffee. Stir to dissolve sugar. Then float chilled whipped cream to the brim of cup and dust with nutmeg.

Irish Coffee for the Party
Yield: 16 servings

>   3 c. Irish whiskey
>   1 c. sugar
>   Coffee, strong, hot
>   Whipped cream, chilled
>   Nutmeg

Pour Irish whiskey into a thermos or crockpot. Stir to dissolve sugar and coffee. Then float chilled whipped cream on top and dust with nutmeg.

Potent Punches

Coffee Caribbean

JOHN E. KALSBECK
Yield: 1 serving

5 ½ oz. coffee, strong, freshly perked
1 ½ oz. Tia Maria
2 T. frozen nondairy whipped topping

Pour coffee into large coffee mugs.
Add liqueur. Cover with topping.

Coffee Caribbean for the Party

Yield: 16 servings

11 c. coffee, strong, freshly perked
16 oz. Tia Maria
2 c. frozen nondairy whipped topping

Pour coffee into large coffee mugs.
Add liqueur. Cover with topping.

Eggnog

PHYLLIS COCKERILL

Yield: 30 servings

    24 eggs, separated
    2 c. sugar
    1 qt. bourbon
    1 pt. brandy
    1 qt. heavy cream
    2 qt. milk
    1 pt. vanilla ice cream, softened
       (more, if desired)

Beat egg yolks and sugar until thick. Add bourbon and brandy and stir thoroughly. Add cream and milk and continue whipping. Add ice cream. Beat egg whites until stiff. Fold in. Refrigerate for 30 minutes before serving. Sprinkle with nutmeg.

Coffee Royale Eggnog

PAT BROWN

Yield: 10 to 12 servings

1 qt. dairy or canned eggnog, well-chilled
1 pt. vanilla ice cream, softened
2–3 t. instant coffee powder
½ t. rum flavoring
Whipped cream
Nutmeg

Combine eggnog, ice cream, coffee, and rum flavoring; blend thoroughly. Pour into chilled cups. Top with whipped cream and a dash of nutmeg. For a 24-serving punch bowl, double the recipe.

Eggnog

UNIVERSITY CLUB OF INDIANA UNIVERSITY
Yield: 8 quarts or 64 4-ounce servings

12 oz. sugar
32 egg yolks
1 t. salt
5 qt. whole milk
2 qt. heavy cream
12 oz. sugar
1 t. salt
32 egg whites
1 T. + 1 t. vanilla
2 qt. vanilla ice cream

Beat together 12 oz. sugar and egg yolks. Add salt. Scald milk and stir in heavy cream. Cook over water, stirring constantly, until mixture thickens or coats a spoon. Cool. Add remaining sugar and salt to egg whites and beat until stiff. Fold in cooled cream mixture. Add vanilla. Whip ice cream lightly and fold into egg mixture. Chill several hours.

Anglo-Saxon Eggnog

BARBARA MEALEY
Yield: 28 4-ounce servings

    6 egg yolks, room temperature
    1 c. sugar
    1 ½ qt. half-and-half
    1 pt. whipping cream
    1 pt. cognac
    1 c. light rum
    6 egg whites, room temperature
    ½ c. confectioner's sugar
    Nutmeg, grated

Beat egg yolks until thick and lemon-colored. Gradually add sugar to yolk mixture. Add half-and-half and cream and beat well. Slowly stir in the cognac and rum. Refrigerate, covered, until very cold. Shortly before serving, beat egg whites until foamy. Gradually add confectioner's sugar, beating until soft peaks form. Gently fold into the yolk mixture. Refrigerate in punch bowl until serving. Sprinkle with freshly grated nutmeg.

Eggnog

DRUSCILLA DEFALQUE
Yield: 40 servings

15 eggs, separated
2 ½ c. sugar
½ t. salt
1 qt. whipping cream
1 qt. whole milk
1 qt. bourbon
1 pt. rye whiskey
½ pt. cream sherry
¾ pt. dark rum
Nutmeg

Blend sugar, salt, and egg yolks together and put aside. Whip cream and let stand. Add milk to egg yolk mixture and blend well. Add bourbon and rye to whipped cream, then the sherry and rum. Blend well. Whip egg whites until stiff, but not dry. Combine whipped cream mixture with yolk mixture, then fold in egg whites. Stir well. Refrigerate for at least 4 hours. Garnish punch bowl with nutmeg.

Café Brulôt

GOURMET GROUP
Yield: 6 servings

Peels of 1 lemon and 1 orange cut into
  1 × ⅛" strips
3 lumps sugar
6 whole cloves
2" cinnamon stick
½–1 c. cognac
¼–½ c. curaiçao
2 ½ c. coffee, fresh, strong

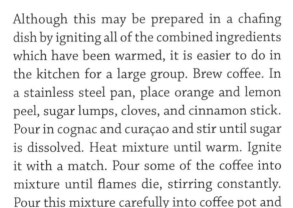

Although this may be prepared in a chafing dish by igniting all of the combined ingredients which have been warmed, it is easier to do in the kitchen for a large group. Brew coffee. In a stainless steel pan, place orange and lemon peel, sugar lumps, cloves, and cinnamon stick. Pour in cognac and curaçao and stir until sugar is dissolved. Heat mixture until warm. Ignite it with a match. Pour some of the coffee into mixture until flames die, stirring constantly. Pour this mixture carefully into coffee pot and stir gently. May be served in demitasse cups or small insulated cups.

Mulled Rum Punch

DONNA WORTH
Yield: 8 servings

    2 qt. apple cider
    ½ c. brown sugar
    12 whole cloves
    4 sticks cinnamon
    8 whole allspice (or ¼ t. ground allspice)
    ¼ t. nutmeg, ground
    1 c. rum

Combine all ingredients except rum in a large pan. Simmer for 15 minutes and strain. Add rum and heat. Do not boil. Serve in mugs with a thin lemon slice.

Hot Buttered Rum

PHYLLIS COCKERILL
Yield: 1 serving

    2 oz. dark rum
    1 or 2 cloves
    1 twist lemon peel
    1 stick cinnamon
    Cider, heated to boiling
    1 pat butter

Put rum, peel, cloves, and cinnamon in mug.
Fill with boiling cider. Float pat of butter on
top. Stir well.

Hot Buttered Rum for the Party
Yield: 16 servings

    2 c. dark rum
    32 cloves
    16 twists lemon peel
    16 sticks cinnamon
    Cider, heated to boiling
    16 pats butter

Put rum, peel, cloves, and cinnamon in mug.
Fill with boiling cider. Float pat of butter on
top. Stir well.

Mulled Cider

ANONYMOUS
Yield: 16 4-ounce servings

2 qt. sweet cider
1 t. whole cloves
1 t. whole allspice
1 3" stick cinnamon
½ unpeeled lemon, thinly sliced
¼–½ c. sugar

Boil all ingredients together for 10 minutes.
Strain and serve hot.

Hot Spiced Cider

UNIVERSITY CLUB OF INDIANA UNIVERSITY
Yield: 2 ½ gallons or 80 4-ounce servings

2 ½ gal. cider
12 oz. brown sugar
10 sticks cinnamon
2 ½ T. whole cloves
2 ½ T. allspice
½ t. mace
1 t. salt
Dash of cayenne

Stir brown sugar into cider. Tie remaining ingredients into cheesecloth bag and place in cider. Bring slowly to the boiling point. Boil 15 minutes. Remove spices. Serve hot.

Potent Punches

Bob's Glögg

JACKIE KALSBECK
Yield: about 24 servings

2 c. red wine (burgundy or claret)
5 cloves
2 c. tawny port
1 T. orange peel, chopped
5 cardamom seeds
1 stick cinnamon
¼ lb. blanched almonds
¼ lb. seedless white raisins
¼ lb. cubed sugar
2 c. brandy

Combine half of wines over low heat. Add orange and spices in cheesecloth. Simmer 20 minutes. Add nuts and raisins and simmer 10 minutes. Remove and discard cheesecloth. Add sugar and brandy. Ignite until sugar is dissolved. Add remaining wine and serve warm, including a few nuts and raisins in each cup.

Wassail Bowl

EVELYN WELLMAN
Yield: 24 4-ounce servings

> 1 gal. apple cider
> 1 c. brown sugar, packed
> 1 6-oz. can frozen lemonade
> 1 6-oz. can frozen orange juice
> 1 T. whole cloves
> 1 T. whole allspice
> 1 t. nutmeg, ground
> 24 sticks cinnamon

In a large kettle, combine cider, sugar, frozen lemonade, and orange juice. Tie cloves and allspice in cheesecloth; add to cider. Add nutmeg. Simmer, covered, 20 minutes. Remove and discard bag. Serve hot in punch cups with cinnamon stick in each cup. This is best made a day or two ahead and allowed to age. For attractive serving, float whole oranges studded with cloves in the punch bowl. If desired, add 2 c. of vodka.

Williamsburg Wassail Bowl

ANONYMOUS
Yield: 20 cups

½ c. water
1 c. sugar
2 sticks cinnamon
3 slices lemon
3 c. cranberry juice
1 c. lemon juice
1 qt. red wine

Boil water, sugar, cinnamon, and lemon slices for about 5 minutes to make a syrup. Strain. Heat, but do not boil, the cranberry juice, lemon juice, and wine. Add syrup to hot wine mixture. Serve piping hot, garnished with lemon slices.

Warm Spicy Wassail

UNIVERSITY CLUB OF INDIANA UNIVERSITY
Yield: 10 quarts or 80 4-ounce servings

    2 ½ lb. sugar
    2 ½ qt. water
    ½ T. whole cloves
    10 sticks cinnamon
    10 allspice berries or heaping
    ¼ t. ground allspice
    5 T. crystallized ginger, chopped
    2 qt. orange juice
    1 ¼ qt. lemon juice
    1 gal. cider
    1 46-oz. can apple juice

Mix sugar, water, and spices. Boil 10 minutes. Cover and let stand 1 hour in a warm place strain. When ready to serve, add juices and cider. Heat quickly to boiling point. May be garnished with floating apples. Serve hot.

Olde English Wassail

MARY HARRINGTON
Yield: 50 servings

    12 small baking apples
    3 c. water
    1 pkg. cinnamon red hots
    1 T. ginger
    1 T. nutmeg
    6 whole cloves
    2 2" sticks cinnamon
    6 allspice berries or ⅛-¼ t. allspice
    1 gal. ale
    3 c. sugar
    1 ½ c. brown sugar, packed
    12 eggs, separated
    1 c. brandy

Wash and core apples. Pare 1 inch of peel
from stem end of each apple. Melt red hots in
1 c. water. Arrange apples in dish, pared side
up, and baste with the flavored water. Bake,
covered, at 350° for 30 minutes or until tender, basting frequently. Combine 2 c. water,

ginger, nutmeg, cloves, allspice, and cinnamon. Cover and bring to a boil, continuing to boil for 10 minutes. Combine ale, sugar, and brown sugar in large kettles. Simmer over low heat until sugar melts. Add water mixture and cook for 10 minutes. Beat egg yolks until lemon colored and thick. Beat egg whites until rounded peaks form. Carefully slide egg whites into punch bowl and pour egg yolks over them. Fold both together. Slowly add hot liquid, stirring constantly. Stir in brandy. Float apples in Wassail bowl. Serve hot.

5

Sans Spirits

Tea for a Crowd

BARBARA MEALEY

Yield: 48 4-ounce servings

    6 c. cold water
    ¼ lb. tea leaves
    3 qt. very hot water (optional)

Bring the 6 c. cold water to a boil. Remove from heat and drop in tea. Stir and steep for 5 minutes. You may now strain this tea concentrate into the hot water (in large coffeemaker) and stir. It is ready to serve.

If you would rather add the tea concentrate to hot water in smaller amounts, use the following proportions: 1 part tea concentrate to 4 parts very hot water. Serve with sugar, cream, and clove-studded lemon slices.

Russian Tea

DEANNA A. YOUNG
Yield: 18 to 20 cups

> ¾ c. sugar
> 1 qt. tea
> 2 sticks cinnamon
> 2 c. water
> 12 cloves
> ¾ t. lemon juice
> 1 qt. orange juice
> 1 qt. pineapple juice

Place first 4 ingredients into a 4- to 5-quart pot and boil for 5 minutes. Then add remaining ingredients, and let boil for 3 seconds. Serve hot or warm. Especially nice on cold evenings.

Russian Tea

DOROTHY MORRISON
Yield: 50 1-cup servings

¾ c. instant tea with lemon and
   sweetening
1 c. orange Tang
¼ t. cinnamon
¼ t. ground cloves

Mix above ingredients well. Store in jar or
canister with tight lid. Add 1 t. of mix to
1 c. of hot water, or measure to suit your
taste.

Hot Cocoa Mix

PETEY MATTHEWS
Yield: 28 8-ounce servings

1 lb. can Nestle's Quik
1 10-oz. box powdered milk (3-qt. yield)
1 8-oz. jar nondairy coffee creamer
1 c. confectioner's sugar

Combine above ingredients and mix well. Store in a large airtight container. To serve stir 3 T. mix into 1 c. hot water.

"500 Festival" Shrub

UNIVERSITY CLUB OF INDIANA UNIVERSITY
Yield: 1 serving

Orange sherbet
Ginger ale, chilled
Mint sprig
Bing cherry, with stem

In a single cup or glass pour ginger ale over
1 scoop of sherbet. Garnish with mint and a
bing cherry with stem long enough to use as
a stirrer.

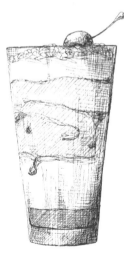

Fresh Lemonade

WANDA NASSER
Yield: 6 servings

> 1 c. fresh lemon juice
> 1 c. sugar
> 1 qt. water

Combine lemon juice and sugar and let stand 10 minutes. Add water and plenty of ice cubes.

Gala Punch

MARGIE GROSFELD
Yield: 25 servings

> 2 qt. sherbet (lime or raspberry
>   recommended)
> 3 qt. ginger ale, chilled

Mix together in punch bowl just before serving.

Frosted Cocktail

ANONYMOUS
Yield: 6 servings

- ½ c. sugar
- ⅔ c. water
- ⅔ c. pineapple juice, unsweetened
- ⅔ c. fresh lemon juice
- 2 T. fresh lime juice
- 2 egg whites, unbeaten
- 4 c. ice, finely crushed (can use blender)

Simmer sugar and water together for 5 minutes. Cool. Shake all ingredients in a shaker or jar until light and frothy. Serve immediately in chilled cocktail glasses.

Yellow Frosted Punch

CLAUDETTE EINHORN
Yield: 40 to 48 servings

   1 48-oz. can pineapple juice
   2 6-oz. cans frozen orange juice
   1 6-oz. can frozen lemonade
   1 qt. pineapple sherbet
   1 qt. ginger ale, chilled

Freeze pineapple juice in can. Remove from freezer about 2 hours before serving and store in refrigerator. Reconstitute all juices and chill. Remove pineapple juice from can and chop with knife. Place in punch bowl. Add other juices. Chop sherbet into small pieces and add. Pour in chilled ginger ale.

Lemon-Lime Punch

UNIVERSITY CLUB OF INDIANA UNIVERSITY
Yield: 50 servings

1 qt. lime juice, strained
1 ⅓ qt. lemon juice
1 lb., 14 oz. sugar
8 qt. cold water

Mix lime and lemon juice with sugar.
Stir until dissolved. Add water and chill.

Yummy Fruit Punch

JAN WAGNER
Yield: 25 servings

2 c. sugar
¼ c. lemon juice
3 c. water
1 6-oz. can frozen orange juice, undiluted
3 bananas, mashed
1 46-oz. can pineapple juice
3 qt. ginger ale, chilled

Heat sugar and water together. Add remaining ingredients except ginger ale. Freeze mixture. When ready to serve, slightly thaw and add 3 qt. ginger ale. Good plain or with rum.

Pineapple Punch

UNIVERSITY CLUB OF INDIANA UNIVERSITY
Yield: 12 quarts or 98 4-ounce servings

¼ c. PLUS 1 ½ t. green tea, bulk
4 ½ c. boiling water
3 c. orange juice
4 ½ c. lemon juice
1 pt. pineapple juice
3 lb. sugar
4 ½ c. water
Water and ice, as needed
4 qt. ginger ale, chilled

Pour boiling water over tea. Brew 3 minutes. Strain through coffee bag or cheesecloth. Cool. Add juices to cooled tea. Boil sugar and water for 10 minutes to make a thin syrup. Chill. Add to the tea mixture. Add enough ice and ice water to make 8 quarts. Just before serving add ginger ale and ice ring.

Cranberry Punch

UNIVERSITY CLUB OF INDIANA UNIVERSITY
Yield: 13 quarts or 104 4-ounce servings

7 qt. cranberry juice
2 qt. lemon juice
4 qt. orange juice
2 lb. sugar

Combine juices and mix thoroughly.
Add sugar. Chill.

Potent Punches

Strawberry Punch

KAREN BAKER
Yield: 1 ½ gallons or 48 4-ounce servings

3 6-oz. cans frozen lemonade
1 10-oz. pkg. frozen strawberries
1 qt. ginger ale, chilled

Dilute lemonade as directed on can. Add strawberries. Add ginger ale and ice just before serving.

Rhubarb Punch

UNIVERSITY CLUB OF INDIANA UNIVERSITY
Yield: 12 quarts or 96 4-ounce servings

20 lb. rhubarb, tender and pink
8–10 lb. sugar
2 gal. water
1 qt. pineapple juice
2 qt. ginger ale

Combine sugar and water; add rhubarb. Cook below boiling point. Strain and chill. Add pineapple juice. Chill. Just before serving add ginger ale.

Potent Punches

Barbara Mealey is the author of *The Cocktail Party Cookbook and Guide.*

Albert W. A. Schmid is the author of *The Old Fashioned: An Essential Guide to the Original Whiskey Cocktail*, *The Manhattan Cocktail: A Modern Guide to the Whiskey Classic,* and *The Hot Brown: Louisville's Legendary Open-Faced Sandwich.*